SHAPING THE EARTH

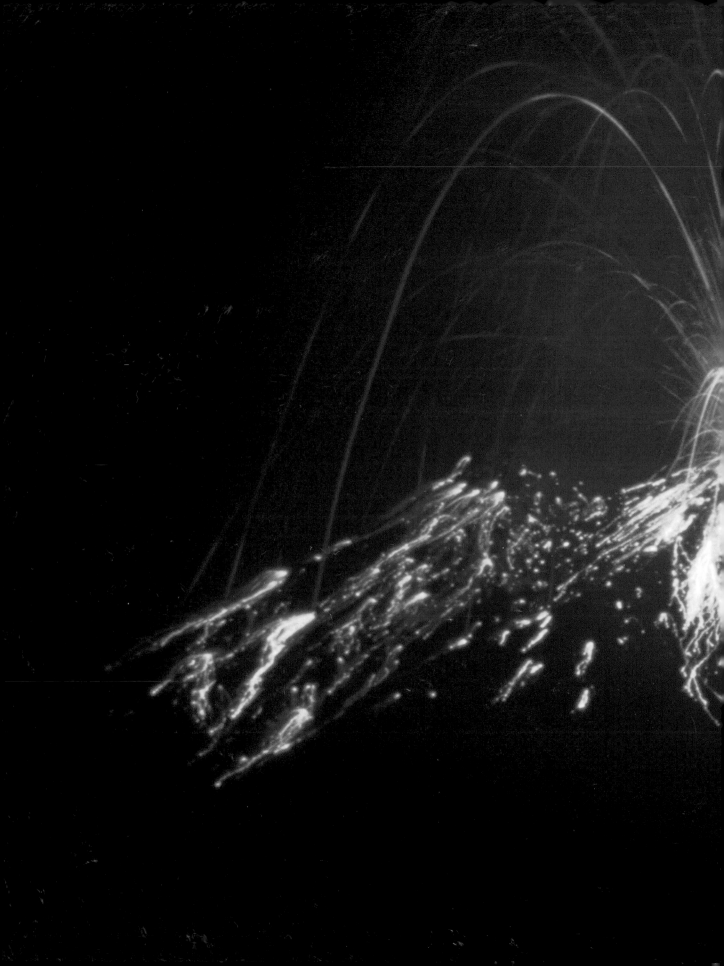

DOROTHY HINSHAW PATENT

ShAPiNG ThE EArTh

PHOTOGRAPHS BY WILLIAM MUÑOZ

CLARION BOOKS / NEW YORK

THANKS TO MARC HENDRIX,
ASSOCIATE PROFESSOR OF GEOLOGY, UNIVERSITY OF MONTANA,
FOR HIS KIND HELP WITH THE MANUSCRIPT

page i: Kilauea's eruptions often involve lava that flows in underground lava tubes and empties directly into the sea.
pages ii-iii: Arenal Volcano in Costa Rica is very active, brightening the sky often with glowing red lava.
page v: Montana's beautiful Mission Mountains.
pages vi-vii: The awesome Grand Canyon provides vital information to geologists about the history of Earth, as well as inspiring visitors with its beauty.

Clarion Books
a Houghton Mifflin Company imprint
215 Park Avenue South, New York, NY 10003
Text copyright © 2000 by Dorothy Hinshaw Patent
Photographs copyright © 2000 by William Muñoz
Diagram illustrations copyright © 2000 by Joyce Powzyk

Additional photograph credits:
Gregory J. Dimijian/Photo Researchers, Inc.: page ii
William E. Ferguson: page 7
NASA: pages 2, 4, 5, 9, 27, 35
Dorothy Hinshaw Patent: pages i, 16, 21, 28, 33, 41, 42, 45, 61, 73, 77, 81
John Reader/Science Photo Library/Photo Researchers, Inc.: page 58
Soames Summerhays/Photo Researchers, Inc.: page 32

The text was set in Rotis Sans Serif.

Book design by Rachel Simon.

Printed in Hong Kong

Library of Congress Cataloging-in-Publication Data
Patent, Dorothy Hinshaw.
Shaping the earth / by Dorothy Hinshaw Patent; photographs by William Muñoz.
p. cm.
Summary: Explains the forces that have created the geological features on the earth's surface.
ISBN 0-395-85691-4
1. Geology Juvenile literature. 2. Geodynamics Juvenile literature. [1.Geodynamics. 2.Geology]
I. Muñoz, Williiam, ill. II. Title.
QE29.P387 2000 550—dc21 99-37093 CIP

DNP 10 9 8 7 6 5 4 3 2 1

This book is dedicated
to the state of Montana
and to Yellowstone National Park,
and all those who strive to keep these places
wild and wonderful.

CONTENTS

Devil's Tower in Wyoming formed from an underground volcanic eruption. As the volcanic rock cooled, it contracted and fractured into columns. Over time, the layers of rock that surrounded the tower eroded away, leaving it to stand alone.

INTRODUCTION

Our planet Earth has been around for 4.5 billion years. During that enormous amount of time, Earth has changed from a lumpy mass of rocks that collided with one another and stuck together into a planet with soaring mountains, plunging canyons, rivers thousands of miles long, and giant oceans.

The forces of geology shaped our planet from the start. But about 3.5 billion years ago, a new and powerful element joined in—life. Living things have changed Earth profoundly, both by their own activities and by their interactions with geological forces.

A few million years ago, a particular life form entered the picture—human beings. At first, humans did little to modify the environment. But around 11,000 years ago, they began to practice agriculture. They cleared wild places and planted fields of grain and replaced forests and brush with pastures and meadows to feed the animals they had domesticated.

This book is about the history of Earth—how it went from its origins in violent collisions and melting heat to what it is today, a constantly changing world of variety and complexity.

Saturn's rings are made up of countless small bits of material, much like the flat rings of planetesimals in the cocoon nebula that surrounded the Sun before the planets formed.

CHAPTER ONE

ROCKY BEGINNINGS

Earth is part of the solar system, with nine planets revolving around the Sun at the center. At the beginning of the solar system, more than 4 billion years ago, there were no planets. The young Sun was surrounded instead by a cloud of dust grains and gas. Astronomers call this a cocoon nebula. The cocoon nebula, however, didn't surround the Sun evenly. It formed a flat disk of material, similar to the rings of debris that orbit around the planet Saturn.

The bits of rocks and dust in the cocoon nebula have been given the name planetesimals. Because there were so many of them and they were so crowded, the planetesimals collided with one another. If they collided without too much force, gravity held them together. Bit by bit, some of the planetesimals grew bigger and bigger as more and more particles joined their clumps. Eventually some of the planetesimals grew to the size of mountains.

The bigger the planetesimals got, the faster and harder they collided. The smaller ones sometimes shattered as a result. But the biggest ones had strong enough gravity to hold on to the bits and pieces from a collision, and they continued to grow. As time went on,

The Hubble Telescope took this near-infared photo of newborn binary stars. A long, thin nebula points toward a companion object at the bottom left, which could be a planet in the process of forming.

the cocoon nebula had fewer and fewer pieces in it, but the pieces were larger and larger. The biggest pieces became planets, and the smaller ones became meteorites.

It's hard for us to imagine the rate of these collisions. Astronomers believe that more than 60 million tons of planetesimals, from the size of dust grains to mountains, collided with our planet each day during its infancy! That meant an almost constant rain of particles smashing into the surface.

Since then, many of the meteorites have collided with the planets, but some still fly through space. Even today, a meteorite sometimes hits Earth, bringing with it clues about the past.

The Melting Planet

As the developing planet Earth got bigger and bigger and its gravity grew stronger and stronger, the planetesimals it attracted hit at ever increasing velocities. Eventually, the heat generated by the almost constant pelting from high-speed fragments melted the planet's surface. As more fragments hit, the layer of molten rock got deeper. Some scientists think that as Earth came close to its present size, it was covered by a sea of lava many miles deep. This is called the magma ocean.

Only a few meteor craters are visible on Earth, since meteors rarely survive the trip through the atmosphere. Fifty thousand years ago, a meteor half the size of a football field hit the ground in Arizona. Most of the meteorite was pulverized, melting sandstone on the ground and sending a shock wave and hurricane force winds, killing all plant life over an area of 500 square miles (1300 square km). Life returned, however, within a few years.

During this violent time, the atmosphere that surrounded the planet was completely different from today's. As the planet grew, the constant rain of planetesimals kept knocking dust into the atmosphere, so the surface would have been shrouded in relative darkness. After the magma ocean formed, both the surface and the atmosphere were very hot. The molten rock gave off large amounts of carbon dioxide gas and water vapor, creating a dense atmosphere with an air pressure at least five times that of today.

Beginnings of Solid Land

As the planetesimals combined into planets and meteorites, fewer and fewer crashed into Earth's surface, so the heat they generated decreased. The magma ocean became thicker, and the surface began to solidify into a patchy crust overlying the liquid rock. This thin, uneven shell floated on top of the magma ocean and was broken by new meteor impacts. Heavy chunks of cooled rock also probably sank from the surface through the magma.

No one knows for sure just when the first lasting rocks formed. Zircon crystals found in Australia appear to be around 4.3 billion years old, so it seems some solid minerals existed by that time. The oldest known pieces of surface rock, found in Canada, date from 3.9 to 3.8 billion years ago.

The hot magma released water, saturating the atmosphere. At first, the surface was too hot for water to form pools. But once it was cool enough, the water vapor condensed into droplets that rained down upon the young rocky crust in torrents. Low spots in the crust soon filled with water, forming Earth's first lakes.

Rain continued to fall, lowering the air pressure and covering the surface of the planet. Here and there, the rims of craters and tops of volcanic islands peeked above the water. Now and then, the red glow from magma rising to the surface reflected from the undersides of the dense clouds in the sky. It was a dim, inhospitable world, its atmosphere heavy with water and carbon dioxide. There was little or no life-giving oxygen.

These rocks in Greenland, dated at 3 billion years old, are among the oldest yet found.

The Moon is the constant companion of the Earth in space.

The Origin of the Moon

The violent collisions of planetesimals that led to the formation of Earth and other planets also resulted in the creation of the Moon. But how? For a long time, scientists puzzled over how the Moon might have formed.

The most popular theory today says that the Moon resulted from the collision of a gigantic planetesimal and Earth. By 4.5 billion years ago, some of the planetesimals had become quite large. They were also moving rapidly. A gigantic one struck Earth. At that time, Earth's crust was thin, and its core had almost formed. When the planetesimal hit, it broke through the thin crust. The impact ripped away part of Earth's mantle and completely destroyed the mantle of the planetesimal. Debris from both mantles sprayed out into space. Much of it fell back onto Earth. But some traveled far enough away to form a ring of fragments around the planet. Then, much in the way Earth formed from debris orbiting the Sun, the Moon formed from the disk of debris that circled Earth.

At first, the Moon orbited close to Earth. But gradually, the Moon's orbit shifted farther and farther away. Even today, the Moon is moving away from Earth at a distance of about an inch a year.

When Earth and the Moon were closer together, the Moon's gravity caused Earth to spin faster on its axis. Soon after the Moon was formed, a day on Earth probably lasted only about six hours. By 4.4 billion years ago, when the Moon was about halfway to its present position, a day on Earth lasted about ten hours, and a month not quite ten days.

CROSS-SECTIONS OF THE EARTH

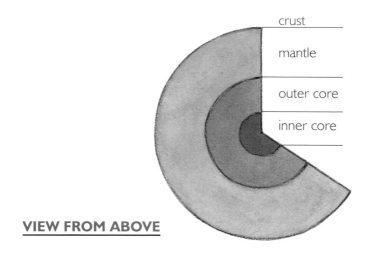

crust

mantle

outer core

inner core

VIEW FROM ABOVE

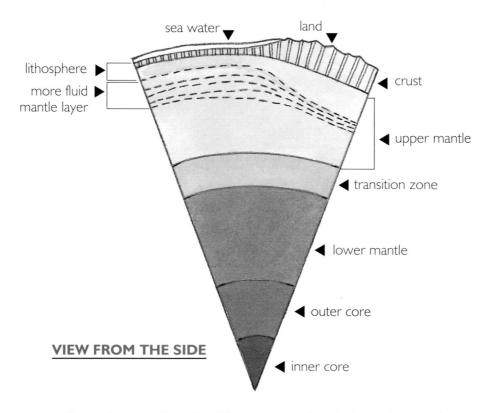

sea water ▼   land ▼

lithosphere ▶

more fluid ▶
mantle layer

◀ crust

◀ upper mantle

◀ transition zone

◀ lower mantle

◀ outer core

VIEW FROM THE SIDE

◀ inner core

These diagrams show the different layers of Earth, from above and
in cross-section, including the lithosphere, which is made up of the
crust and the uppermost part of the mantle.

CHAPTER TWO

FORMING TODAY'S EARTH

No one knows for sure how the young Earth became the rocky ball of land and water, teeming with life, that we know today. Scientists debate the ancient causes, but they agree on some of the basics.

Layers of Earth

The very early Earth had a liquid-magma surface and probably a solid core. Today, the situation is different. Earth's surface is covered by a layer of rock called the crust. This layer is thickest on the continents. The continental crust averages 28 miles (45 km) thick. Under the oceans, the crust has an average thickness of only 5 miles (8 km). The continental and oceanic crusts are very different. The continental crust is made up mainly of rocks rich in the elements silicon and aluminum. The thinner but denser oceanic crust contains more calcium, iron, and magnesium than does the continental crust.

Underneath the crust is a layer called the mantle. The mantle is the planet's thickest section, making up 83 percent of its volume. The mantle is complicated in structure, with several layers. The upper part is mostly solid, while the lower mantle appears to be made of molten rock.

Earth's core lies beneath the mantle. The core is very different from the mantle. The mantle has plenty of silicon and magnesium, while the core is made up of an alloy (combination) of the metallic elements iron and nickel. The outer core is liquid metal. The inner core is solid because of the tremendous pressure created by so much overlying material.

How did Earth transform from a planet with a liquid-magma surface to one with a liquid interior and solid core? Several factors are key to this big change. For one thing, heat is produced within Earth by the decay of radioactive elements. And under high pressure, as beneath the planet's surface, iron melts at a lower temperature than rocks containing silicon (silicates). The iron separated from the silicates when the heat melted the iron, and gravity helped carry it toward the center of the young planet. As the planet cooled, the extreme pressure deep within solidified the inner core. Geologists believe that the core formed around 4.4 billion years ago.

The Lifeless Earth

The planet may have had its basic inner structure more than 4 billion years ago, but things on the surface weren't calm. Planetesimals were still hitting the surface at a high rate. The heat of impact sometimes vaporized the oceans, which re-formed when the water recondensed and fell once again in torrents. Large impacts also blasted away part of the atmosphere, so that neither the air pressure nor the content of the atmosphere was constant. The Moon was much closer, too, causing enormous tides.

We'll never know if life appeared and then died out during this long period of instability. We do know that the planet remained lifeless for hundreds of millions of years. Ocean waves lapped the barren shores, and rainfall washed exposed broken rock and dust into the sea. The sun rose

The Complex Mantle

The mantle has several layers of its own. The boundary between the crust and the mantle is quite narrow in geological terms, perhaps a few hundred yards (or meters) thick. The uppermost layer of the mantle is quite rigid. The crust plus the more solid part of the mantle is called the lithosphere (rocky sphere). The lithosphere is thicker under land—up to a few hundred miles (several hundred kilometers) under the older parts of the continents—than under the oceans. There, it may be as thin in places as 31 miles (50 km).

Underneath the lithosphere lies a more fluid layer of the mantle. Then, still deeper, the mantle thickens again. These combined layers, which reach to a depth of from 186 to 250 miles (300–400 km), are called the upper mantle. Then comes another transition zone, followed by the lower mantle, which begins at 416 miles (670 km) deep. The lower mantle is quite uniform in its composition. It extends all the way down to 1,802 miles (2,900 km) beneath the surface, where it meets the core.

and set, rose and set, volcanoes erupted, islands were created and destroyed. Now and then, a large planetesimal hit the surface, creating a new crater and throwing dust into the atmosphere. On and on, the hazy skies rested on a lifeless planet.

Life's Beginnings

Despite years of research, the beginnings of life on Earth remain a deep mystery. Some scientists believe that the building blocks of life, called organic compounds, arose on Earth through chemical processes. Others think the organic materials came from space.

What are these vital life chemicals? Organic compounds are defined as chemicals that are based on carbon. This element is the foundation for life on Earth. In 1953, Stanley Miller of the University of California, San Diego, decided to see how organic compounds might have arisen on the early Earth. He joined two glass flasks with tubing. In one, he placed water, representing the early ocean. Then he pumped gases (hydrogen, methane, and ammonia) into the other, larger flask. At the time, scientists thought that these gases made up Earth's early atmosphere. Then Miller boiled the water so that the vapor would mix with the gases, and he mimicked lightning, the most likely source of energy on early Earth, by zapping the mixture with electricity.

Within a week, the water changed color, developing reds and yellows from a variety of organic compounds. Among these were amino acids, the building blocks of proteins, which are one of the most important classes of life chemicals. Before Miller's work, people had thought that making organic compounds was a difficult process, but he showed that it was actually quite easy.

Scientists now believe that the early atmosphere consisted mainly of carbon dioxide, water, and nitrogen instead of Miller's mixture. Today, new theories abound on the question of how life began. Some scientists believe that the organic molecules for life came from outer space. It turns out that organic compounds are common in the universe. A quarter of Halley's comet is made up of them, and 10 percent of tiny interplanetary dust (smaller than 1/250 of an inch, or 0.1 mm) consists of organic material. Others, however, believe the concentration of cosmic material that actually reaches Earth's surface is too small for life to have arisen from it.

A new theory proposes that life began deep in the ocean at the hot vents of undersea volcanoes. The vents spew out a mixture of gases from inside Earth. When the hot gases meet the cold ocean water, chemical reactions leading to organic compounds could occur. Today, a variety of life forms survive around such vents.

We will probably never know for sure how life came to be on Earth. We do know that by 3.5 billion years ago life began leaving its traces as fossils. Since these fossils consist of fully formed cells, the basic units of life, we know that life itself must have had its origins long before then. But the process occurred so long ago on a planet so different from what it is now that any concrete evidence of how it occurred has been lost. However it began, life is one of the major forces that has shaped our planet in the past and that continues to shape it every day.

Some scientists believe that the origins of life may have come from outer space. Comets, like Hale-Bopp, can contain organic compounds.

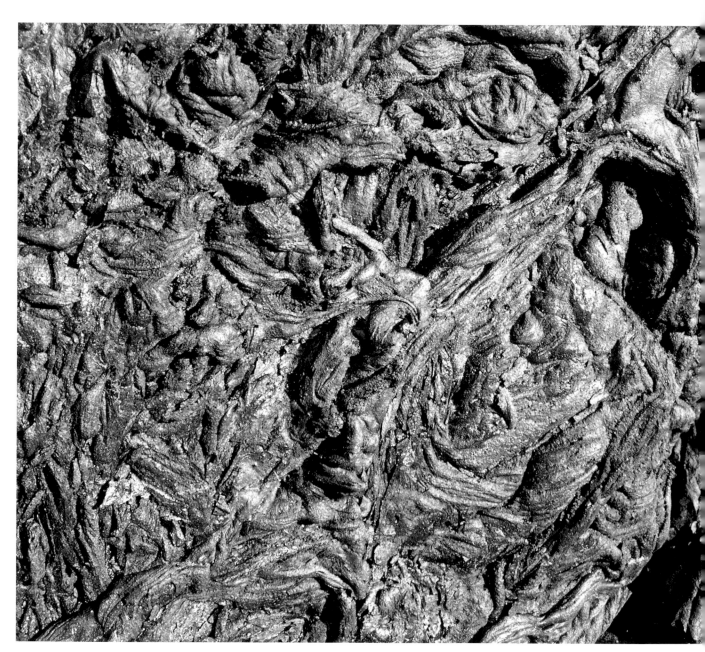

Fresh lava still erupts from volcanoes, as it did during the early days of our planet.

CHAPTER THREE

THE RESTLESS EARTH

As Earth was developing its final size and its present layers, the surface was changing, too. In addition to the craters formed from impacts of planetesimals and meteors, the liquid from the mantle broke through thinner parts of the crust in places, pouring more liquid rock onto the surface. When such eruptions occurred beneath the sea, some of these undersea mountains eventually peaked above the surface, forming islands. On land, the hardened lava became mountains. Earth's surface was developing variety—oceans and land, high points and low ones.

The Unsettled Continents

Sometimes scientists take a long time to accept ideas that challenge old beliefs. Even when evidence supports a new but different theory, many years may pass before scientists come around to the new way of thinking.

One of the best examples of this difficulty in accepting new concepts is plate tectonics. Until the 1960s, geologists believed that the surface of Earth was solid. They thought that the present continents had formed just where they are today. The idea that the continents might have moved around over time had been suggested, but no one paid much attention.

But in 1910, Alfred Wegener, a German scientist, began exploring the idea that the continents had shifted. Like some before him, he noted that the shape of the coast of South America matched up remarkably well with that of Africa. The two looked almost like adjoining pieces of a jigsaw puzzle.

In 1911, Wegener learned that similar fossils had been found in South America and in Africa, thousands of miles away. Today, these two regions have very different animals. But fossils reveal that early species in South America and Africa were similar, evidence that these two continents might have been joined long ago. Mainstream geologists thought there might have been a land bridge between the two continents during a past era, which animals could have crossed. But Wegener concluded from the shapes of the coastlines that Africa and South America had been joined and therefore were once home to the same plants and animals. Later on, a split occurred, and the continents began drifting apart. The plants and animals then evolved separately, in response to their changing environments, leading to the very different creatures that live on the two continents today.

In 1912, Wegener published a book, *The Origins of Continents and Oceans*, in which he provided plenty of evidence for his theory, which included much more than fossils and the complementary appearance of the coastlines. He pointed out that mountains like the Alps were made up of crumpled layers of rock, folded as if they had been pressed from the sides. A very important piece of evidence noted by Wegener is the difference between the rocks forming the continental crust and those of the oceanic crust. The continental crust is lower in density than the oceanic crust. Wegener argued that the less dense continental crust floated on top of more dense semiliquid rock underneath, similar in

The golden lion tamarin is a monkey that lives in South America. Like other New World monkeys, it can use its tail for grasping branches. African monkeys lack this ability.

composition to the oceanic crust. The differences between the two types of crust also disproved an old explanation of how the ocean basins formed, which said that they consisted of ancient continents that had sunk. If that were the case, both types of crust should be similar in composition.

Wegener found that the layers of rock on the African and South American coasts matched each other, just like the fossils and the coastlines. This was another important piece of evidence: If the rocks were the same type, with the sequence of their layers matching, they must have once been joined. By studying the fossils carefully, Wegener estimated that the continents had been joined during the Devonian period, about 300 millions years ago. Wegener gave the name Pangaea, which means "universal land," to the huge continent of long ago.

Rock-Hard Geology

Even the greatest geologists of the time did not accept Wegener's theory. What could cause enormous masses of rock to float over the surface of Earth? No one, including Wegener himself, could find a mechanism. For this reason, geologists stubbornly resisted Wegener's ideas, despite the strength of his evidence.

In the early 1960s, research methods led to the discovery of new information about our planet's history that made Wegener's ideas seem not so outrageous after all. It became possible to sample rocks from the Mid-Atlantic Ridge, on the floor of the Atlantic Ocean. Scientists found that the rocks forming the middle of the ridge were very young. The farther out from the middle they sampled, the older the rocks became.

These findings showed that the floor of the Atlantic Ocean was formed by volcanic activity releasing lava along the ridge and spreading to the sides. If the floor of the ocean had been spreading, making it wider, then the continents on either side must have been separating, growing farther apart. Wegener had been right.

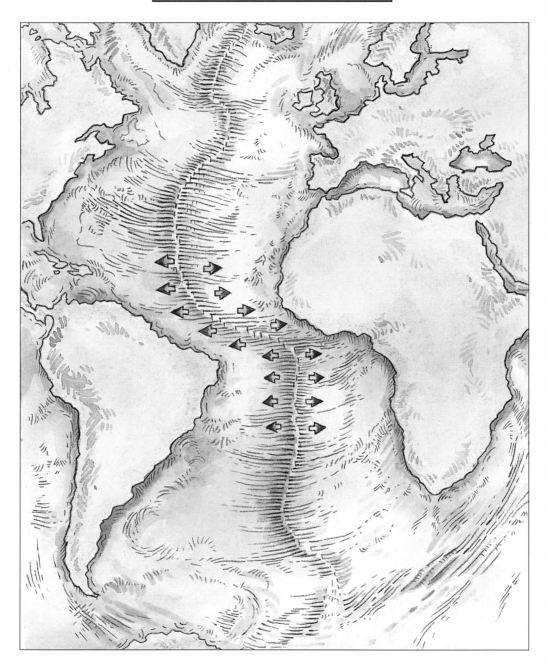

The arrows indicate the direction of sea floor spreading along the Mid-Atlantic Ridge.

But for some geologists, old ideas die hard. Despite this very strong evidence, it wasn't until the late 1960s that Wegener's ideas were generally accepted. Since then, his theories have been refined and the mechanisms by which the movements of the continents take place have been uncovered.

The Wandering Continents

A major stumbling block in accepting Wegener's theory was the belief that the upper mantle was solid rock. Geologists didn't see how any force could be strong enough to move through it. But now we know that the upper mantle is quite hot and therefore flexible. We also understand that even the most solid rock, given enough time and pressure, can bend. These realizations have helped shape the new geology of plate tectonics.

Plate tectonics states that the surface of Earth is covered by a shell of rock called the lithosphere. The lithosphere is made up of the crust and the very top part of the mantle. It varies greatly in thickness. The lithosphere has cracked in places and become divided into about ten pieces called tectonic plates, which float on the surface of the more dense but fluid layer beneath. Imagine a bathtub full of honey with blocks of wood floating on top.

When new lava erupts along the oceanic ridges and comes to the surface through cracks in the lithosphere, it pushes the plates bearing continents apart.

Geologists are working on reconstructing how the continents have moved over time. The farther back they look, the harder it is to find evidence. So far, they agree that around 500 million years ago two giant continents graced our planet's surface. What is now South America, Africa, India, Australia, and Antarctica is called Gondwanaland. The other

PLATE TECTONICS

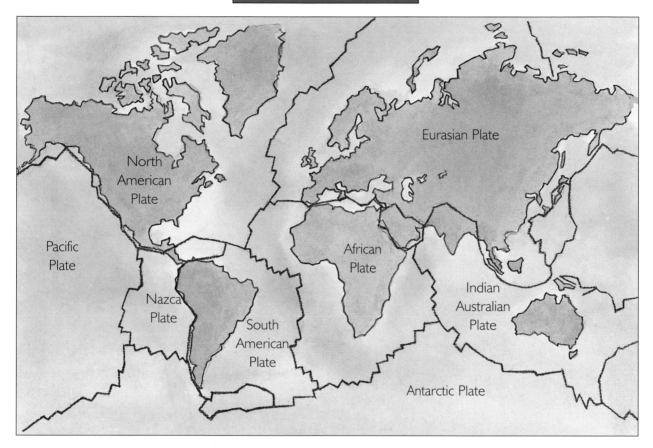

North American Plate

Eurasian Plate

Pacific Plate

African Plate

Nazca Plate

Indian Australian Plate

South American Plate

Antarctic Plate

The red lines indicate the borders of Earth's tectonic plates. The larger plates are labeled.

Islands in the Sea

The eruptions deep in the ocean along the oceanic ridges aren't the only deep-sea volcanic activity. Here and there, but not located along the edges of the tectonic plates, are hot spots, where lava erupts from the mantle through the plates. The Galápagos Islands, the Hawaiian Islands, and other oceanic islands formed and are still forming at such hot spots. Altogether, about forty hot spots erupt to Earth's surface, most of them through the thinner oceanic crust.

Hot spots are associated with especially hot regions of the upper mantle, not with weak spots in the plates. From the surface, it appears that the hot spot is moving. But actually, the hot spot stays put and affects different parts of the crust as the plates move over it, forming different islands. The Hawaiian Islands are a good example. The plate carrying the islands moves slowly to the northwest, so the oldest island is the one farthest northwest—Kauai. From Kauai, the islands form a string that extends toward the southeast. The places where the hot spot penetrated the crust, called volcanic centers, are about 100 miles (160 km) apart. Oahu was the second island to form, followed by Molokai and Maui. The big island of Hawaii still rests over a hot spot. Every year, new land forms on the southern side of the big island. During recent decades, the lava has destroyed homes and roads on its way to the sea.

OPPOSITE: New land, such as this black beach on the island of Hawaii, is being constantly formed even today by volcanoes.

ABOVE: The mountains along the Na Pali coast of Kauai are old enough to be clothed by trees and plants.

25

continent, made up of present-day Asia (other than India), Europe, and North America, is called Laurasia. Gondwanaland lay in the south, with Laurasia to the north.

Over time, the movements of tectonic plates brought the two continents together to form one enormous land mass. All Earth's continents were joined about 210 million years ago into the supercontinent Wegener called Pangaea. As the plates shifted, Pangaea broke up, and the present-day continents formed. The outlines of today's continents took shape about 100 million years ago. At that time, the continents were closer together, but they were drifting apart, floating atop their own plates toward their present locations.

Near the Continental Divide in Montana, layers of rock have been folded and broken so that the horizontal layers now stand as vertical rocks.

Making Mountains

Sometimes, a plate carrying solid land crashes into another plate that also carries land. The one continental mass pushes against the other, causing layers of rock to fold and break. All this takes place over very long periods of time, lasting up to millions of years. The results of such relentless pressure can be spectacular. Mountains like the Himalayas, where the tallest peak on Earth reaches skyward, were formed in this way.

At the edges of some continents, such as along the Pacific coast of South America, a plate of dense oceanic rock meets up with a plate of lighter continental rock. Instead of colliding with the continent, the heavier oceanic plate slides beneath it. This process is called subduction. The pressure from the two plates meeting still makes mountains, but in this case they are formed as material scraped off the down-going slab joins the edge of the continental plate. The sliding of one plate underneath the other also forms a deep trough under the sea. Some of the deepest parts of the ocean are near the edges of the continents.

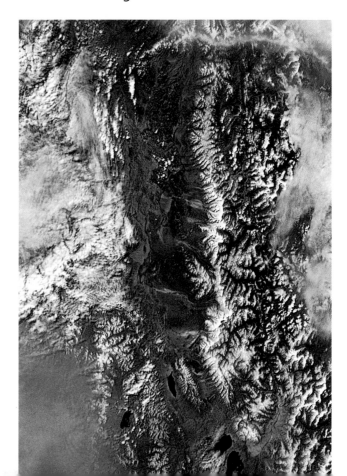

Skylab took this photo of the Himalaya Range.

A chain of volcanoes in the Cascade Range marks the Pacific coast from southwestern Canada into northern California.

CHAPTER FOUR

PLANET OF FIRE

Because the plates move so slowly, we don't normally see evidence of their activity. Even over generations of human life, the continents seem to be rooted in place. But the discovery that they do indeed move and that they ride atop surface plates has helped explain some aspects of our planet that can affect people in very direct ways.

Volcanoes in Action

Volcanoes are a dramatic display of our restless Earth. There are 1,500 active volcanoes on our planet. Many of these are close to cities and towns—500 million people live near them.

Volcanoes form in three ways. We've already seen how lava pours out along the ocean ridges, where the plates are moving apart. We've also found out how islands are created when hot spots punch holes through the plates that move over them.

Volcanoes also form where an oceanic plate comes up against a thicker but less dense continental plate and is subducted, sliding beneath it. The subducting slab melts as it enters the hotter zone in the mantle, and the melted rock is spewed out of volcanoes that form a long chain along the edge of the continent. The Pacific coast of the United States is marked by a line of volcanoes where the Pacific (oceanic) plate is being subducted under the North American (continental) plate. Mount Rainier near Seattle, Washington, and Mount Shasta in California are two well-known volcanoes in this chain. Mount St. Helens, which erupted so violently in 1980, is another member of this group.

Geologists call this chain of volcanoes and the others that surround the Pacific Ocean the Ring of Fire. The Ring of Fire traces the subduction zones of the Pacific plate as it slips under the plates that surround it. The volcanoes of Japan, the Philippines, and other Asian islands, as well as those of New Zealand, are part of the Ring of Fire. The Ring of Fire reaches as far north as the Aleutian Islands in Alaska and as far south as Antarctica.

RING OF FIRE

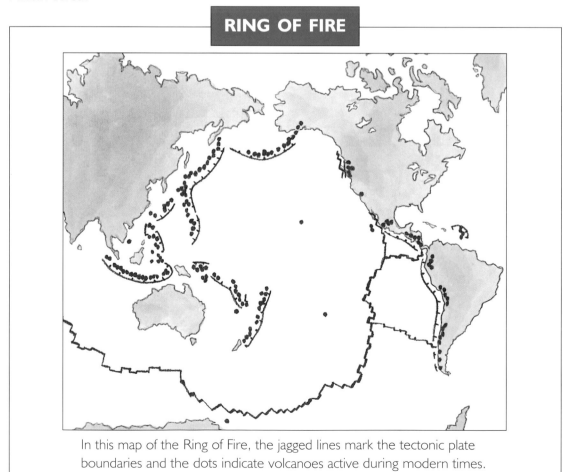

In this map of the Ring of Fire, the jagged lines mark the tectonic plate boundaries and the dots indicate volcanoes active during modern times.

Kinds of Eruptions

When we think of a volcano erupting, we picture glowing red molten rock spewing up in the center of a volcanic cone, then flowing down the sides as rivers of liquid rock. Some volcanoes do erupt in this dramatic fashion, but many don't. The Hawaiian volcano Kilauea doesn't have a cone-shaped top like a typical volcano. Kilauea's eruptions can still be spectacular. During some of its eruptions, blobs of liquid lava are thrown skyward along cracks in the surface, forming brilliant red fountains. But much of Kilauea's lava also flows hidden underground, through a network of tunnels called lava tubes, emerging along the edge of the island and cascading into the sea to form new land. In 1991, I visited Kilauea, stepping out onto the still-warm lava. It glowed red in the cracks beneath my feet. At the shore, the lava poured into the sea, forming great clouds of steam. I walked along the youngest land on the island, a black sand beach formed when the fiery lava hit the water and shattered into tiny bits.

Volcanoes that erupt with lava flows usually cause little loss of human life. People can get out of the way of the slowly streaming lava in time. Towns and villages may be destroyed, but the people can find homes elsewhere.

Another kind of eruption is far more dangerous. Materials deep in Earth are under a great deal of pressure from the overlying layers, and gases dissolve readily in liquids under pressure. When magma rises into the crust, where the pressure decreases, gases dissolved in the magma come out and expand, just as gas fizzes in a soda bottle when you open it, releasing pressure. The expansion of the gases presses against the solid rock of a volcanic cone. The pressure can become so great that the volcano explodes, shattering rock into an immense cloud of ash that rises miles into the atmosphere and may completely circle Earth.

Explosive eruptions can also result in deadly pyroclastic flow, a hot cloud of gas, ash, and rock that can race down the side of the volcano and sweep across the landscape at 200 miles (320 km) per hour. Pyroclastic flows can kill instantly, engulfing people in deadly gas and searing heat before they can escape. The eruption of Mount Vesuvius in southern Italy in A.D. 79 killed around 2,000 people in the city of Pompeii and also destroyed the nearby town of Herculaneum. Pyroclastic flow from the 1980 eruption of Mount St. Helens in Washington State flattened forests for miles around. Many of the 57 people killed in the eruption were overcome by the pyroclastic flows.

The Shaking Earth

I grew up in the San Francisco Bay Area, where residents are often reminded that our planet is restless. The start of a day can seem normal in

Kilauea can erupt with spectacular shows of spurting and flowing lava.

every way. All of a sudden, a rumbling sound is accompanied by swaying light fixtures. Cupboard doors fly open. The floor shakes, making walking a challenge. Then the rumbling and shaking stop, and everything seems normal once again, except for the lingering fear that a show of such unpredictable power brings. Mild earthquakes like this are familiar in places like California, Japan, and Central America. Even smaller earthquakes are very common. Geologists are able to detect around 600,000 earthquakes every year. Most of these are too small for people to notice, but sensitive machines can pick them up. Sometimes, however, Earth moves violently, bringing death and major destruction.

Plate tectonics makes sense of earthquakes. Earthquakes can occur where one plate is moving underneath another. Plates can also adjoin one another along edges called fault lines. For example, the famous San Andreas Fault in California, which has brought about many serious earthquakes, runs through the state from southeast to northwest. Its

Thirteen years after the eruption, the landscape around Mount St. Helens is still scarred.

southern end is near Indio, a small desert town north of the Salton Sea. From there, it passes through the Mojave Desert, then northward, roughly parallel to the coast, until it approaches the San Francisco Bay Area. The fault runs right underneath the city of San Francisco, crossing underwater just outside the Golden Gate. From there, it continues northward under the Pacific Ocean, close to the coastline. Most of northern California is east of the fault. But a couple of small pieces of land are on the west side.

The tectonic plate on the eastern side of the San Andreas Fault is moving slowly to the southwest, while the plate on the western side is on its way northwest. As the plates move slowly in different directions, pressure builds up along the fault. The movement of the plates is jerky, not continuous. When the stress between them becomes too strong, they slide roughly against each other, shaking the ground. In 1906, a great earthquake struck the San Francisco Bay Area. The place where the San Andreas Fault gave way, called the epicenter of the quake, was north of San Francisco, near Point Reyes. There, the two plates scraped and lurched past each other by as much as 21 feet (6.4 m). The shaking lasted less than two minutes, but the results were disastrous. In the city of San Francisco, buildings collapsed and fires broke out, lasting three days and destroying much of what was left.

Geologists have studied the San Andreas Fault most intensively at the town of Parkfield, in southern California. On average, a quake occurs every 22 years, when the two faults slip by each other a distance of about 24 inches (60 cm). Bit by bit, the Los Angeles area, which is on the Pacific plate, is moving northward. Some people imagine that Los Angeles will one day crumble into the Pacific Ocean. Instead, it will move slowly, one earthquake at a time, northward.

The movements along this fault have led to some interesting

differences along the coast. The geology of the Point Reyes area, in Marin County north of San Francisco, is very different from the nearby land. Point Reyes is on the Pacific plate, so it is a visitor from the south, separated from the main landmass of California by the San Andreas Fault. Like Los Angeles, Point Reyes is on its way north.

Southern California is riddled with faults, some of which can be seen from the air. In this photo, Santa Monica is in the north (top middle), and Oceanside to the south. A fault line can be seen in the dark area of mountains near the upper right, running diagonally toward the upper middle.

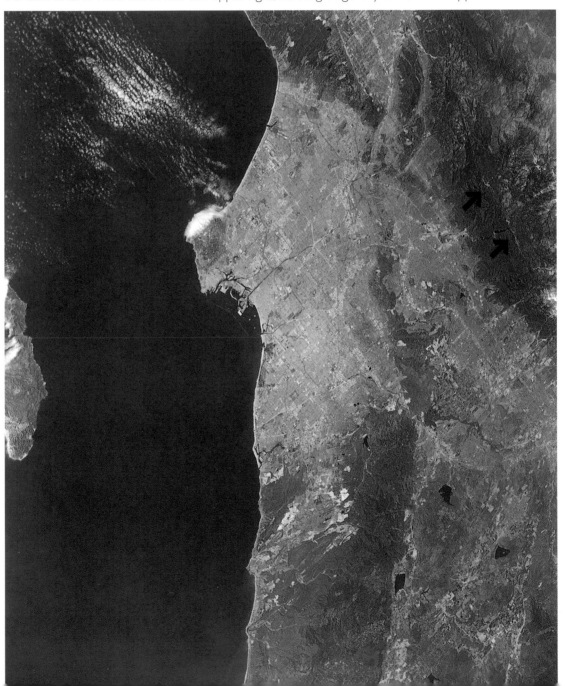

Colter's Hell

In the winter of 1807–08, an adventurer named John Colter set out to
bring fur-trapping Indians to Manuel's Fort, built where the Yellowstone
and Bighorn Rivers join in present-day Montana. Colter ended up traveling
deep within what is now Yellowstone National Park, a region of spouting

ABOVE: The thermal pools of Yellowstone National Park show that hot rock lies close to the
surface there.

geysers, steaming hot springs, and hot pots of bubbling mud. At the time, people dismissed his stories as exaggerated lies, and historians still debate how far he actually traveled. However, it seems clear that he was the first European American to see these natural miracles. Appropriately enough, the region was dubbed Colter's Hell.

Yellowstone is unique for the scope and variety of its thermal features, hints on Earth's surface of the enormous heat that lurks underneath all our feet. The heart of the park is actually a gigantic caldera, a huge volcanic crater formed by the collapse of a volcanic cone. Over a period of 2.1 million years, three calderas developed above an unusual hot spot. (Only a few hot spots lie underneath the thick continental crust.) The first caldera formed in what is now Idaho, to the west of Yellowstone. As the continental plate moved westward, the second caldera appeared farther east, and the third, where much of the thermal activity occurs, lies right in the center of the park.

The past eruptions of the calderas left behind devastation greater than we can easily imagine. The first eruption spewed 2,400 times as much volume of volcanic rock and ash into the atmosphere as the 1980 eruption of Mount St. Helens. The ash drifted all the way to what is now California to the west and Iowa to the east. In places, several feet of ash buried the landscape.

As the North American plate moves slowly westward, the hot spot under Yellowstone appears to be moving ever so slowly to the northeast. Scientists have tracked its history all the way from Nevada to its present location. If the plate keeps going in the same direction, Montana, North Dakota, and parts of Canada will eventually pass over the hot spot. The journey would take millions of years and could create some real geological fireworks along the way.

Glaciers once covered much of Europe and North America. Today, they are limited to regions near the poles and in the high mountains, such as Alaska.

CHAPTER FIVE

AGES OF ICE

Earth could be called a planet of fire and ice. The slow, grinding passage of ice, miles thick, has shaped its surface every bit as much as the fiery eruptions of volcanoes. Beginning about 60 million years ago, Earth cooled down, and thick layers of ice began to form. By 35 million years ago, ice had buried Antarctica. Seventeen million years ago, Greenland was blanketed by glaciers. Finally, about a million years ago, the cold enveloped North America and Europe in ice. The ice advanced and retreated across the continents about ten times, once every 100,000 years or so.

What Causes Ice Ages?

Scientists have studied the ice ages intensively. Most agree that the cooling was brought about by a decrease in carbon dioxide in the atmosphere. Carbon dioxide is called a greenhouse gas, for it traps heat from the sun. When carbon dioxide and other greenhouse gases increase, as they recently have, the average temperature on the planet goes up. When there is less carbon dioxide, the temperature falls.

What brought about the decrease in atmospheric carbon dioxide?

One theory states that when grasses evolved and covered miles and miles of land, they removed enough carbon dioxide from the atmosphere to trigger the ice ages.

Scientists can't agree on an answer to this puzzling question. Many believe that periodic changes in Earth's orbit around the Sun reduced the strength of sunlight striking the planet's northern region. Less warmth meant more ice, resulting in the buildup of glaciers that brought about the ice ages.

Other scientists feel that the ice ages are somehow tied to the formation of the Himalayas, which occurred at about the same time the ices ages began. Large amounts of minerals eroding from the mountains might have combined with carbon dioxide to form limestone. This chemical process could have removed enough carbon dioxide from the atmosphere to bring about the cooling. Others think sediment from the erosion entered the Indian Ocean and buried huge quantities of marine plants, killing them and entombing the carbon dioxide they contained. The uplifting of mountains could also have affected the circulation of Earth's atmosphere in a way that cooled northern regions. Over time, the Plateau of Tibet went from a warm tropical lowland teeming with life to a cold, barren plateau 14,000 feet (4,267 m) above sea level, with the frigid Himalayas towering over it.

An Icy Blanket

A glacier isn't just a thick layer of ice. It is a river of ice, flowing slowly over the landscape, scraping, grinding, and shaping the land as it moves along. Glaciers take tens of thousands of years of consistently cool temperatures to form. First of all, large quantities of snow must fall during the winter. Summers need to be cool enough that some of the snow doesn't melt. If you live in snow country, you may have wondered why it sometimes takes so long for the snow to melt even when the air

A glacier is a slow-moving river of ice.

Glacial ice is eerie blue in color. This Alaskan glacier moves slowly into the sea, breaking off huge chunks, which become icebergs.

temperature is above freezing and the sun is shining. Frozen water doesn't melt easily. It takes 80 times as much heat to turn ice into water as it does to raise the temperature of water just one degree, from 32°F to 33°F (0°C to .56°C).

Just as it takes a lot of warmth to melt water, persistent cold is required for glaciers to form. But once they are established, glaciers tend to endure for a long time. Major changes in climate are required both to form glaciers and to melt them.

As a glacier develops, the layers of snow compact under the weight of the snow buildup on top. Snowflakes combine into granules, which then fuse to form solid ice. The ice in a glacier takes on an eerie shade of blue.

Before the icy mass becomes a glacier, it must become thick and heavy enough to move in response to gravity. Ice is a very stiff material, more than a million million times as stiff as water, so it takes a lot to get it moving. Glaciers move slowly, usually no more than a few feet a year. As they move, the ice within changes constantly as crystals melt and refreeze and are rearranged by the movement. The pull of gravity brings about much of the movement, but other factors also enter in. Often, the friction of the glacier moving over rock melts a thin layer so the glacier slips and slides on the thin, watery cushion. Such slipping can account for as much as 90 percent of a glacier's movement.

Carving the Landscape

The stiffness of glacial ice has powerful effects on the landscape. Glaciers can carry huge boulders along for miles and miles. They can scour and polish the landscape, removing all the soil and sweeping it along, leaving behind smooth barren layers of rock.

The evidence of ancient glaciers is easy to see in the Rocky Mountains. As the ice flowed over rocky ridges and bumps between mountains, the pressure these barriers exerted on the ice melted it. The water then seeped into cracks and crevices, where it froze again. Since water expands about 10 percent when it freezes, the rock around the cracks was shattered and carried along by the glacier. This process widened narrow canyons between mountains and smoothed their contours to form beautiful U-shaped valleys.

As the climate warmed, glaciers began melting faster than they formed. Bit by bit, the leading edges receded farther and farther. As a glacier melts, it dumps all the rocky debris it has carried from afar into piles and ridges called moraines. Meltwater from the glacier can carry

This U-shaped valley in Glacier National Park in Montana was formed by glaciers.

debris from the moraines across the landscape, creating rocky plains that extend from the base of the glacier.

It's difficult to picture just how huge glaciers were in North America. At their greatest extent, they covered 10 million square miles of land that today harbors only a few small glaciers high in the mountains. Glaciers covered the land where the city of St. Louis, Missouri, now swelters in

44

The sun glints off the melting face of an Alaskan glacier. In the foreground is a moraine made of rocks and pebbles.

summer heat. They reached into what we know as southern Illinois. Glaciers were thousands of feet thick. The Mission Range in western Montana shows dramatic evidence of just how deep the glaciers were. The southern peaks of the Missions are jagged and dramatic, formed by rock lifted up by a fault line. Glaciers helped form dramatic craggy valleys below the peaks. But farther north, the Missions become smooth, rounded mountains. During the last ice age, these peaks were completely buried under a glacier that was thousands of feet thick.

Glaciers also left smaller signs of their passage. Grasslands in parts of the country are dotted by small ponds called potholes. These ponds formed

The top of snow-covered Mount Calowakin, which used to be called Mount Harding, was not covered by glaciers. Its ridges are still sharp. The smaller mountain in front, with the rounded top, was shaped by glaciers.

when huge chunks of ice carried by a glacier were left in place. The ice was very heavy, so when it finally melted completely, it left a depression in the ground. Potholes are important to wildlife, for they provide breeding and feeding grounds for waterfowl such as ducks and geese.

Prairie potholes like this one in Wisconsin are important breeding grounds for ducks, geese, and other birds.

Glacial Lake Missoula

My present home lies on a flat spot on the side of a mountain overlooking the floor of the Missoula Valley in Montana. Every summer, the grasses in the meadow across the street turn a delicate tan as the hot sun dries them out. The climate here borders on the desert—an inch or two less rain every year and our forests might die out.

It's hard for me to believe that all this land once lay under several hundred feet of water. About 15,000 years ago, a large part of western Montana was actually a lake bigger than Lake Erie and Lake Ontario combined. The lake inundated several valleys, including the present-day Missoula and Mission Valleys. This enormous lake was almost 2,000 feet (610 m) deep. It developed during the last ice age, when a glacier formed an ice dam across the path of what is now the Clark Fork River in northern Idaho. Over a period of 3,000 years, the lake grew and shrank, grew and shrank, until the dam broke.

48

The resulting flood shaped the land for hundreds of miles to the west. Water poured out with ten times the force of all the rivers in the world today put together. It ripped away everything in its path, stripping off 200 feet (61 m) of topsoil from northern Idaho and eastern Washington. Then it found the Columbia River gorge and raced toward the Pacific Ocean. To this day, land along the river is quite barren, its soil ripped off and carried to the sea by waters from hundreds of miles away.

For decades, no one could figure out how to explain these barren landscapes or the huge ripple marks on rocks in Montana, some as tall as three-story buildings. Other geological features in the area were also puzzling. In 1923, geologist J. Harlan Bretz concluded that a flood from a giant lake had created the unusual landscapes. Bretz, however, couldn't say where the lake had been, and fellow geologists shrugged him off. As far back as 1910, another geologist, Joseph Pardee, pinpointed the Missoula area as the source for all that water. Only in the last 30 years or so have geologists come to agree that such a huge body of water indeed had existed and broken free to create a new landscape so long ago.

ABOVE: This sign on a hill overlooking the Mission Valley shows how high the water of Glacial Lake Missoula was.

The Appalachian Mountains, like this stretch in West Virginia, are now tree-covered rounded hills instead of the rocky peaks of millions of years ago.

CHAPTER SIX

THE EVER-CHANGING LAND

Volcanoes and glaciers aren't the only forces that sculpt the land. Every day, the forces of water and wind are at work, making tiny changes in mountains, valleys, and plains. The result over time is great drama like the Grand Canyon or the haunting beauty of Arches National Park in Utah.

Earthquakes and volcanoes can change the landscape dramatically in moments. But most geological change takes place over thousands or millions of years, such as the uplifting of mountains by tectonic forces. Mountains are lifted over millions of years, and it takes millions of years to destroy them, too.

The Appalachian Mountains

As the supercontinent Pangaea was forming, the east coast of North America was moving toward rather than away from Europe and North Africa. As the plates collided, they folded the layers of rock along the coast to form a new range of mountains. When they were young, these mountains were probably at least as tall as the Alps are today. We call what is left of these once towering peaks the Appalachian Mountains. To residents of the Rocky Mountain West, the Appalachians hardly qualify as mountains. They are rounded hills covered with forests.

The process by which these once high, craggy mountains became gently rolling hills was largely the gradual, insistent work of wind and water, bit by bit washing and blowing away tiny pieces of rock and soil.

As mountains are worn away by wind and water, the material removed has to go somewhere. Over millions of years, the eroded minerals can come to rest on rocky surfaces and build up, layer by layer, until they form high plains. Geologists can study these layers to learn details about how Earth has changed over time.

The Colorado Plateau

The Colorado Plateau is a unique region that extends through parts of Arizona, Colorado, Nevada, New Mexico, Utah, and Wyoming. Over 300 million years ago, this land formed the bottom of a salty sea. The sea came and went, came and went, over vast stretches of time, leaving layers of sediment.

As the layers formed, the remains of living things joined the mineral deposits. The more sediment collected, the heavier the layers became. The weight of the layers above compressed the layers below, turning them into rock. Rocks that are formed in this way, as sediments that accumulate layer by layer, are called sedimentary rocks.

The record of hundreds of millions of years of Earth's history was locked in the sedimentary layers of the Colorado Plateau. Luckily for geologists, about 5 million years ago the Colorado River and the smaller rivers that feed it began to carve their way through the Colorado Plateau. Snowmelt from the mountains brought torrents of water in the spring. The climate was dry, so the land had few plants whose roots could hold the ground together.

Bit by bit, the rivers cut into the plateau, bringing to light the many layers of the region's geological history. The result today is spectacular canyons—Bryce, Zion, and, biggest of all, the Grand Canyon. Geologists can study the layers of rock exposed in the canyons and read changes that occurred in the landscape like pages in a book of time.

The Courses of Rivers

Rivers affect the land in many ways. Every river starts out as a modest stream that forms from a spring, rainfall, snowmelt, or melting glacial ice.

The awesome Grand Canyon provides vital information to geologists about the history of Earth as well as inspiring visitors with its beauty.

Gravity draws the water down slopes, and small streams empty into the developing river, making it larger and more powerful as it continues on its course. Rivers cut through rock and make V-shaped canyons as they hurry down mountain slopes. When they cross over a layer of hard rock into a layer of softer stone, rivers carve away the softer material, creating waterfalls.

When a river reaches the lowlands, it slows down. Since its current is not as strong, rocks and soil carried from above are deposited as sandbars and islands. Where a river bends, the current cuts away at the bank on the outside of the bend, making the bend gradually more pronounced. The twists and turns of the river are called oxbows or meanders. Sometimes a river will straighten itself out by cutting across one of these bends, forming an island. If the old river channel is cut off from the new one, an oxbow lake can form.

Rivers may flood when rainfall or snowmelt increases. Some rivers flood every year, depositing rich soil from higher elevations onto the land. Much of the best farmland in the world is in river valleys for this reason.

As a river gets closer to the sea, it slows down even more. Here, it deposits more sediment, creating a triangular area called a river delta. The river divides into small channels that connect it with the sea. River deltas, where salt and fresh water mix, are some of the richest areas for plants and animals. Many marine animals such as fish and shrimp use delta areas for breeding.

The Subtle Wind

Compared with water, wind is a minor force in creating landscapes. But it can have striking and sometimes important effects. Wind carries tiny particles of dust and sand. When these particles rub against soft rock, they can break parts loose and polish what is left.

Where sand or soil are loose, the wind can have more dramatic effects. When a grain of sand is disturbed by the wind, it hops along over the surface, stirring up other sand particles. As the wind picks up, the sand blows faster, and more and more grains join in flight. A full-blown sandstorm can blot out the sun and completely change the landscape in just a few hours.

When farmers plow their fields, wind can pick up the topsoil and whisk it away, leaving the land poorer. The effect of wind on the land became grimly clear during the 1930s. The westerly winds were stronger than usual at this time, and the land was dry. Where once strong-rooted grasses had held the soil in place, farmers plowed up the ground, exposing the rich topsoil to the wind. Tons of valuable topsoil blew away, and thousands of families were forced off their now unfruitful land. In May of 1934, so much dust had been raised by the wind and blown eastward that midday in New York City, far from the Midwestern fields, looked more like twilight.

Sedimentary rock is formed as layers of material are deposited at the bottom of a body of water and then turn to stone.

Wind and Water Together

When wind and water join to form tropical storms such as hurricanes, they can have dramatic effects on landscapes. I visited Cape Romain National Wildlife Refuge in South Carolina in the spring of 1989. Bulls Island, a part of the refuge that borders the Atlantic Ocean, was blanketed by a dense forest that shaded every inch of ground underneath it. The giant trees arched over the dirt road that led to the shore. A sandy beach bordered the ocean and was lapped by modest waves.

Hurricane Hugo made landfall in autumn of that year. It hit Bulls Island directly as a 22-foot-high (6.7 m) tidal surge, a giant wave fraught with power. Two and a half years later, I returned to the island.

Every tree that still stood was broken off raggedly at about the height of the wave. Sunlight shone onto the ground through the battered limbs, and an amazing variety of birds that hadn't been there before sang loudly. The trees may have been wounded, but the opening of the forest had provided homes for a new variety of life.

I wandered down to where the beach had been. The island had lost more than 20 feet (6.2 m) of sand, destroying the old beach completely. The new beach was narrow and littered by big dead trees lying on their sides, their fans of roots reaching toward the sky. When I examined the trunks closest to the water's edge, I saw tiny barnacles covering the trunks, making homes for themselves. Bulls Island showed me that in what we see as nature's destruction, just as much is created as destroyed.

ABOVE: The damage from Hurricane Hugo was still visible on Bulls Island more than two years after the storm.

These tablelike formations that cover much of the shallow waters of Shark Bay in Western Australia are called stromatolites.

CHAPTER SEVEN

THE LIVING PLANET

Of all the planets circling our Sun, only Earth teems with life. Scientists study how living things adapt to their physical environments, how they deal with desert drought, arctic cold, mountain steepness. But living things don't merely adjust to their surroundings, they also change them. They shape Earth's surface every bit as much as the dramatic physical forces of earth, water, and wind.

Life Alters the Planet

No one knows when life, this powerful landscape-changing force, began on Earth. The oldest fossils discovered so far date from 3.5 billion years ago. It's amazing that these have been found, for they consist of single cells, visible only with a microscope.

Some ancient cells secreted calcium carbonate, forming large stony masses coated by living cells. These formations survive and continue to form today. They are called stromatolites. Some stromatolite fossils are more than 3 billion years old.

The blue-green algae that make up these colonies look similar to bacteria. But, unlike bacteria, they can make their own food using energy from the Sun. Blue-green algae and plants alike contain a chemical called chlorophyll. Chlorophyll enables cells to use the Sun's energy to break down carbon dioxide. The carbon is combined with water to build the molecules of life, and the oxygen from the carbon dioxide is released into the air. This process is called photosynthesis.

At the time blue-green algae appeared, Earth's atmosphere consisted mostly of carbon dioxide and water vapor, so the materials these cells needed to grow and reproduce were easy to come by. Bit by bit, eon by eon, the thriving colonies of stromatolites and other kinds of blue-green algae multiplied, releasing more and more oxygen into the atmosphere. The concentration of oxygen in the air increased. Over the course of a billion years, the amount of carbon dioxide was reduced, and oxygen increased until it became a significant influence in shaping both life and the planet.

What Oxygen Does

As the oxygen content of the atmosphere increased, living things first became adapted to its presence, then began to use it as a source of energy. Most living things today depend on oxygen to fuel their bodies. During the day, plants release oxygen into the atmosphere. But at night, they remove some of it for use as an energy source.

Oxygen is a very reactive chemical. The only reason oxygen continues to exist in our atmosphere is that it is being constantly replenished by photosynthesis. Because it reacts so easily, its effects on physical materials is as dramatic as its influence on life. Oxygen feeds the flame of fire as well as the explosive burning of gasoline to run motor vehicles.

Once oxygen became common in the atmosphere, its effects on geological processes were striking. The layers of red rock that create the

The trees and other plants that form forests, such as this one in Costa Rica, are vital to the survival of all life on Earth, including human beings.

The red color of rock formations of Arches National Park in Utah and other beautiful areas of the western states comes from minerals containing oxidized iron.

breathtaking beauty of America's southwestern landscapes are made of oxidized iron (iron combined with oxygen). Rocks older than 2 billion years rarely show rust-colored oxidized layers. Instead, the layers are usually blue or gray.

The First Ice Age

In chapter 5, we discussed what might have brought about the ice ages that started 60 million years ago. But Earth endured a much earlier ice age around 2.3 billion years ago, around the time that blue-green algae had been spewing oxygen into the atmosphere long enough to replace

significant amounts of carbon dioxide. Many scientists believe it was this life that brought about the first ice age.

Back then, the Sun was a cooler star than it is now. But even though the Sun was giving off less heat, Earth was kept warm by its blanket of heat-holding carbon dioxide. Then along came life, blue-green algae that gobbled up the carbon dioxide and replaced it with oxygen. When the concentration of carbon dioxide became low enough, the atmosphere could no longer hold in the heat, and the planet cooled off until giant sheets of ice covered much of Earth's land. Over time, the Sun gradually warmed until the power of its heat overcame the grip of the ice, and the glaciers receded.

A lone mangrove grows near the Florida shoreline. Normally, these plants form thickets along the shoreline, their branched aerial roots breaking up incoming waves and providing homes for many kinds of animals.

Life's Interactions

On Earth today, life is probably the greatest influence in shaping the planet, from its effects on the atmosphere to the ways it modifies the surface. The roots of trees and grasses hold the soil in place over miles and miles of forest and grassland. Along coastlines, salt-tolerant plants such as mangroves protect the shoreline from erosion. The decay of dead organisms adds chemicals to the soil that wouldn't be there without the activities of life.

Under our feet, earthworms do the work of aerating the soil. We may not realize it, but healthy land teems with these busy workers. In most soils, half the weight of animal life consists of earthworms. An average acre of ground contains a half ton of earthworms. Where the soil is rich and fertile, 12 tons of earthworms can inhabit an acre. In an acre, earthworms bring anywhere from 2 to 100 tons of material to the surface each year, pulling leaves down into the soil and depositing rich worm castings on the surface. Worm burrows help drain the soil and bring life-giving oxygen to other animals and to the roots of plants.

Have you ever wondered why archeologists must dig into Earth to find ancient ruins? The activities of earthworms are a major reason. In just a

Ferns are among the first plants to colonize lava in Hawaii.

Beavers Really Are Busy

Bacteria, lichens, plants, and worms aren't the only living things that modify Earth's surface. Large animals can also have an impact. Beavers are among the most dramatic landscape modifiers.

Beavers are truly sculptors of the land. These large rodents feed on the leaves, twigs, and bark of trees, and they use the trees they cut

ABOVE: Beaver dams create ponds that serve as flood control as well as homes for many plants and animals.

down with their sharp teeth to make dams as well as lodges where they can raise their families. Once the dam slows the flow of water, the beaver builds a protected lodge in the new pond. The entrance is underwater, making it very difficult for a predator to get in.

Because the dam holds back water and creates a pond, it also raises the level of water in the surrounding soil. The abundant moisture encourages the growth of water-loving plants such as aspen and willow, which the beavers like to eat. Nearby meadows also thrive because of the higher water level in the soil. Beaver dams provide natural flood control, regulating the release of water so that it doesn't all rush down in a fast, heavy stream during the spring. A stream without a beaver dam may be almost dry by late summer, but a dammed stream continues to flow, slowly releasing some of the water held back by the dam.

When beavers are around, other wildlife also thrives. One study showed that 153 kinds of small mammals lived in beaver-pond habitat, while only 50 could be found where there were no ponds. Many kinds of birds and fish, too, make their homes in beaver ponds.

Lichens gradually eat away the surface of rocks.

few years, these busy creatures bring several inches of soil up to the surface, burying things that used to lie on top.

From Rock to Soil

Like water, ice, and wind, life can help break down rock into soil. After lava has flowed over the land, destroying life on the surface, it slowly becomes the home for new life. Wind and water bring bits of sand, dead leaves, and other materials, which are deposited in cracks in the rock. Within just a few years, plants grow in the crevices. Their roots reach into the tiniest cracks beneath the surface, expanding them and crumbling the rock. When these plants die and decay, they provide nutrients for the next generation of plants. Bit by bit, the rock breaks down and organic material is added. The lava flow becomes fertile new soil.

Boulders left standing in grasslands by ancient glaciers may seem to be stones of the ages that will remain forever. But the clumps of gray, green, and brilliant orange lichens that grow on them are ever so slowly breaking them down, dissolving their minerals to establish a foothold.

A Magic Transformation

Living things on Earth's surface can gradually bring about geological changes. And after they die, they themselves can be changed chemically to produce valuable resources for humans. In prehistoric times, when much of what is land today was flooded by shallow seas, single-celled floating algae thrived in the waters. When the algae died and were buried by clay, heat and pressure brought about changes in their chemicals, resulting in a gooey material called kerogen. Inside the warm earth, the kerogen broke down into simpler, more fluid molecules, creating a chemically complex mixture we call oil. Under the right geological conditions, oil collected in rocky reservoirs within Earth, where humans could tap it. Similarly, coal formed from plants that lived in freshwater swamps. Again, temperature and pressure resulted in chemical changes that created a fuel source for humans. The modern industrial world depends heavily on both oil and coal, remnants of the abundant life of former times.

You can see the layers of rock that overlie this West Virginia coal seam.

This power plant in Wyoming is clearly releasing chemicals into the atmosphere.

CHAPTER EIGHT

HUMANS CHANGE THE PLANET

Of all life forms inhabiting Earth today, none has as great an effect on its development as our own species. We are able to modify the environment so that we can live anywhere on the planet except within fiery volcanoes. We plow the soil, dam the rivers, log entire forests, and pour thousands of chemicals into the air and water. Since the Industrial Revolution began in the eighteenth century, the concentration of carbon dioxide in the atmosphere has increased by almost 30 percent. We have modified 40 to 50 percent of the planet's surface to suit our needs and desires, and our population continues to grow and demand that still more land be taken over. Even places left to nature, where people have intruded least, are affected by such human-caused alterations in the environment as increased levels of pesticides and climate changes.

The pace of environmental change that humans have imposed on Earth is too fast to enable most natural systems to adapt. Thus we now have a laundry list of environmental problems, including poisoned water supplies, huge mudslides that bury entire villages, and growing deserts. In addition to local difficulties, we have helped create planetwide problems, such as global warming, that could force us to alter drastically the way we live.

Changing Waters

Life on Earth is based on water. Most of the human body consists of this vital fluid. Without a supply of clean, fresh water, living things perish. Water is also a key to geological processes and to climate.

Humans now use half the planet's fresh surface water for their own purposes, mainly for farming. Around the world, 36,000 dams hold back rivers in order to provide water for irrigation, flood control, and electrical power. Many more dams are under construction or on the drawing board. Once-powerful rivers such as the Colorado and the Nile are almost entirely used up before they enter the sea. Where great floods deposited life-giving silt on rich delta land, mere trickles are all that survive because of human demand.

Damming of rivers also creates reservoirs that flood canyons and valleys, creating artificial lakes, and changing the landscape and local climate. Water evaporating from the large surface increases the humidity of the air. Because water warms up and cools down so slowly, the large mass of water moderates the climate.

From Wildlands to Croplands

Thousands of years ago, people acquired food by hunting game and gathering wild plants. The biggest cultural change in the history of our species came when we learned how to domesticate wild animals and plants. It seemed easier to grow crops and raise animals deliberately, close to home, rather than rely upon the chancy process of going out and looking for food.

Most of the shrublands and forests of Switzerland are gone, turned into grasslands for grazing animals such as these goats.

Our efforts to raise our own food have profoundly changed the surface of Earth. In the European Alps, the highlands once covered by shrubs became grassy pastures, grazed upon by sheep and goats. Much of the vast prairies that covered the midsection of North America have become pastures for cattle and sheep. Wild species have diminished on these lands dominated by domesticated animals.

The rest of the prairies and a vast proportion of other land in the world have been converted from wildlands to croplands. From 1700 to 1980, the

Furrows that run vertically down a slope carry water rapidly downward, taking precious topsoil with it.

area of cultivated land around the world increased by 466 percent! In many tropical countries with growing human populations, forests are cut down so that the land can be used to grow crops.

All this comes at a price. When forests are turned to croplands, the local climate tends to become warmer and drier. Intensive agriculture leads to increased erosion, which results in lower fertility of the soil. Native species of plants and animals are pushed out, and many have become extinct. Fertilizers and pesticides contaminate the water that runs off farmers' fields, harming living things far away.

San Francisco Bay

San Francisco Bay was once a haven for an incredible variety of wildlife. The Sacramento and San Joaquin Rivers brought abundant water into the bay every year, and the bay's shores were lined with wetlands where fish, birds, and many other creatures reproduced. Today, the natural parts of the bay have almost completely disappeared, and the water from the rivers that feed it is used for crops such as rice and cotton.

As a result, wildlife populations have plummeted. The decline in living things is seen all the way from the tiny single-cell plants that float about in the water to birds, mammals, and fish both small and large. In 1959, more than 1.5 million water birds were counted in the bay. In 1997, just over 320,000 were found. In the 1960s, the bay was a haven for fish such as striped bass, with 3 million bass counted. Today, there are fewer than 600,000. Some fish have just about disappeared—salmon, which used to spawn in the Sacramento River, once numbered more than 100,000. In 1991, only 191 showed up.

The takeover of the land by people has also resulted in the loss of freshwater animals and land-living creatures whose homes are away from the shore. When I was growing up in the bay area, I used to catch San Francisco garter snakes in Golden Gate Park and red-legged frogs in creeks across the bay. Now, both of these species are endangered and may die out completely.

Fortunately, people are trying to save the bay. Many fish are now protected by the Endangered Species Act, and water quality standards have been raised. More fresh water is going into the bay, and ponds once used for drying salt are being converted into wetlands where wild things can thrive again. The bay can never return to its former abundance, but at least some of its health is being restored.

Humans have completely taken over the once-wild shores of San Francisco Bay.

The Berkeley Pit in Butte, Montana, was once one of the biggest copper mines in the world. Now it holds a deadly lake filled with water containing chemicals so poisonous that nothing can live in or on it.

Digging and Building

Besides needing food and water for survival, people require homes to live in and materials for building. Forests are cut down to provide wood, and enormous mines are dug to acquire minerals like copper and silver. The freeways that cover miles and miles of potential habitat for wild species also serve as deadly barriers to travel for animals.

Cities such as Chicago can create many environmental problems. Fortunately, efforts in recent years have greatly reduced this city's pollution of Lake Michigan.

Cities provide an unnatural environment that alters both landscape and climate. Hills are flattened and terraced to make homesites. Marshes are filled in for houses and shopping malls, destroying the breeding grounds for countless species. Concrete and asphalt soak up the warmth of the sun, increasing the temperature by several degrees within the city.

The Future

As long as human population continues to grow, the demand that more land be converted to our use will increase. Scientists are trying to figure out ways to minimize the negative effects of turning natural landscapes into ones that serve humankind. They are also developing a new science called restoration ecology that can help bring back natural habitats to environments damaged by human activities.

Increased awareness of the effects of chemicals like herbicides and

Shanghai is one of China's fastest growing cities; it is also among the world's most polluted.

pesticides may lead to finding ways to limit their use. Some industrialized countries are working to reduce the amount of carbon dioxide they release into the atmosphere. Most developing countries, however, feel they cannot afford expensive equipment to limit the amount of harmful chemicals that are discharged into the environment.

The problems created by the increasing demands we put on our beautiful planet provide enormous challenges to all of us who live on Earth.

Wind and water can create strange formations as they erode different kinds of rocks.

By the Next Millennium

A thousand years may seem a lot to us, but it's just a brief moment in the life of our planet. Many famous American landmarks, such as the Grand Canyon and Mount Rushmore, will look pretty much the same as now. Erosion destroys approximately an inch of rock surface of the Rushmore images every 10,000 years. By the year 3000, however, our planet will have undergone some slightly larger changes. San Francisco and Los Angeles will be about 170 feet (52 m) closer together than they are today. The coastal mountains of southern California will be perhaps 15 inches (38 cm) taller. Meanwhile, on the other side of the continent, North America will be 82 feet (25 m) farther apart from Europe. And if global warming continues to melt polar ice, there will be even more noticeable changes. Some oceanic islands could disappear under the waves, and coastal cities could be threatened or even abandoned.

GLOSSARY

alloy A combination of two or more metals.

caldera A big crater formed when a volcano explodes or collapses.

chlorophyll A green chemical in plants that helps them capture the Sun's energy.

cocoon nebula A cloud of dust grains and gas that forms a flat disk surrounding a star such as our Sun; over time, it can be transformed into planets.

continental crust The surface layer of Earth that underlies the continents.

crust The solid layer of rock that covers the surface of Earth.

element The basic unit of chemistry and physics, such as iron, chlorine, sodium, and silicon. Elements can't be broken down into smaller units by ordinary chemical means.

epicenter The place where tectonic plates slip past one another, causing an earthquake.

fault line The line between two tectonic plates, where earthquakes can take place.

glacier A thick layer of ice that doesn't melt during the summer. Glaciers flow slowly downward, pulled by gravity.

Gondwanaland One of two big continents that existed about 500 million years ago. Gondwanaland consisted of South America, Africa, India, Australia, and Antarctica.

greenhouse gases Gases, such as carbon dioxide, that act like a greenhouse, holding heat in the atmosphere.

hot spot A place in Earth's mantle where lava rises to the surface and can break through an overlying tectonic plate.

inner core The center of the Earth. Even though it is hot, the inner core is solid because of great pressure from the overlying rock.

kerogen A gooey material produced by heat and pressure acting on the remains of ancient single-celled algae. Kerogen becomes oil under the proper conditions.

Laurasia One of the two big continents that existed about 500 million years ago. Laurasia consisted of Asia (other than India), Europe, and North America.

lava Liquid magma that has poured out onto the surface of the planet.

lithosphere The crust plus the solid part of Earth's mantle.

magma Liquid rock under the planet's crust.

magma ocean The sea of liquid lava that once covered Earth's surface.

mantle The layer of the planet under the crust.

meteorite A rocky or metallic chunk of material created by collisions of planetesimals.

moraine A pile of rocks left when a glacier melts and retreats.

oceanic crust The part of Earth's crust that lies beneath the oceans.

organic compounds Chemicals that contain the element carbon. These are the molecules of life.

outer core The part of Earth that lies between the mantle and the inner core.

Pangaea The supercontinent that developed about 210 million years ago when Laurasia and Gondwanaland joined.

photosynthesis The process by which plants capture the energy of the Sun by combining water and carbon dioxide to make sugars and release oxygen.

planetesimals Large chunks of rock and metal that formed by joining of particles in the cocoon nebula.

plate tectonics The process by which the pieces of Earth's crust move on top of the liquid mantle below.

pothole A pond formed after big chunks of glacial ice melt, leaving a depression in the ground.

pyroclastic flow A mass of very hot volcanic ash, rock, and gas that rolls down the side of a volcano, destroying everything in its path.

Ring of Fire The circle of volcanically active sites that surrounds the Pacific Ocean.

sedimentary rock Rock formed in layers by particles that have settled on the floor of a body of water.

silicon An element that combines into hard compounds called silicates.

stromatolites Stony masses of calcium carbonate formed by blue-green algae.

subduction The process by which one tectonic plate slides beneath the edge of another.

tectonic plates The pieces of lithosphere that float on top of the liquid mantle.

volcanic centers Places where hot spots break through the crust.

volcano A hole in the crust through which lava and gases are ejected.

FURTHER READING

BOOKS

Good, John M., and Kenneth L. Pierce. *Interpreting the Landscape: Recent and Ongoing Geology of Grand Teton and Yellowstone National Parks.* Moose, Wyoming: Grand Teton National History Association, 1996.

Lauber, Patricia. *Volcano: The Eruption and Healing of Mount St. Helens.* New York: Simon & Schuster, 1986.

Van Rose, Susan. *Volcano & Earthquake* (Eyewitness Books, No. 38). New York: Knopf, 1992.

Vogel, Carol G. Shock *Waves Through Los Angeles: The Northridge Earthquake.* New York: Little, Brown, 1996.

Walker, Sally M. *Volcanoes: Earth's Inner Fire* (A Carolrhoda Earth Watch Book). Minneapolis: Carolrhoda Books, 1994.

MAGAZINE ARTICLES

Davidson, Keay, and A. R. Williams, "Under Our Skin: Hot Theories on the Center of the Earth," *National Geographic,* January 1996, 100–111.

Earth magazine had a special issue entitled "Origins," February 1998. Articles deal with Earth's core, the structure of the planet, origins of life, and so forth.

Gore, Rick, "Living with California's Faults," *National Geographic,* April 1995, 2–35.

Grove, Noel, "Volcanoes: Crucibles of Creation," *National Geographic,* December 1992, 5–41.

Matthews, Samuel W., "Ice on the World," *National Geographic,* January 1987, 79–103.

Vitousek, Peter M., "After the Volcano," *Natural History,* June 1997, 49–53.

White, Robert S., "Ancient Floods of Fire," *Natural History,* April 1991, 51–60.

WEB SITES

http://www.amnh.org/rose/hope/ The official site of the Hall of Planet Earth at the American Museum of Natural History

http://geology.usgs.gov/index.html United States Geological Survey Web page. Latest information about earthquakes and links to other USGS pages.

http://www.platetectonics.com A great site for plate tectonics.

http://www.glacier.rice.edu Rice University Web site dealing with glaciers in Antarctica.

http://dir.yahoo.com/Science/Earth_Sciences/Geology_and_Geophysics/Glaciology This site will give you current Web sites that deal with glaciers.

http://dir.yahoo.com/Science/Earth_Sciences/Geology_and_Geophysics/Seismology This site gives current Web sites dealing with earthquakes.

http://dir.yahoo.com/Science/Earth_Sciences/Geology_and_Geophysics/Plate_Tectonics Current plate tectonics sites.

INDEX

Page numbers in *italics* refer to illustrations.